Frederick J. (Frederick James) Allen, Frederick James Allen

A Topical Outline of English History

Frederick J. (Frederick James) Allen, Frederick James Allen

A Topical Outline of English History

ISBN/EAN: 9783741186844

Manufactured in Europe, USA, Canada, Australia, Japa

Cover: Foto ©ninafisch / pixelio.de

Manufactured and distributed by brebook publishing software
(www.brebook.com)

Frederick J. (Frederick James) Allen, Frederick James Allen

A Topical Outline of English History

OF

ENGLISH HISTORY

INCLUDING REFERENCES FOR LITERATURE

FOR THE USE OF CLASSES IN HIGH SCHOOLS
AND ACADEMIES

BY

FREDERICK J. ALLEN, A.M.

PRINCIPAL OF THE HIGH SCHOOL, MILFORD, N.H.

*Preëminent among the stories of the nations stands
the story of the Anglo-Saxon race.*

BOSTON, U.S.A.
D. C. HEATH & CO., PUBLISHERS
1895

Norwood Press:
J. S. Cushing & Co. — Berwick & Smith.
Norwood, Mass., U.S.A.

PREFACE.

HISTORY has more sides than the gold and silver shield. No writer has given us all that is best upon any period or subject. The method of the following pages, carefully developed, and tested in the class-room with gratifying results, enables the student to appropriate the best to be found in many books. It covers the entire field of English history, and aims to fill that place in its study which the laboratory manual fills in chemistry.

The topics are more complete than can be found in any one text-book. They are placed upon the left side of the page, with numbers upon the right referring to the pages of the latest editions of standard school histories. The arrangement is both chronological and related, special effort being made so to group facts that relation and result may be clearly understood. Careful attention has been given to dates, and constant sight of topic and date, rather than any committing to memory, fixes both in mind. In the case of sovereigns, the pages given mark only the beginnings of the reigns; in other cases the references include all of value to be found.

This book is a result of practical teaching, and those teachers who have seen it in preparation have warmly advised its publication.

It is, first of all, a class-book, taking away no individuality of teacher or pupil, and being especially adapted to working purposes. The author's method has been as follows : —

Have a variety of histories in the class ; let each pupil use a copy of the *Topics* and one or more text-books, with works of reference constantly at hand. Let the class keep note-books, also, in which may be written concise statements on the daily lessons, especially useful for re-review. This stimulates investigation, and arouses in each member of the class a desire to bring what others do not.

It also serves as a test in selection and discrimination. For instance, the author once asked his class for results of the reign of William the Conqueror, and twenty-five definite results, positive and negative, were promptly given.

Names of writers have been combined with the historical topics, because it is believed that literature is best understood when seen in its proper setting of political and social history ; and the knowledge so gained will serve to direct further reading and research. In most cases one representative book is given with each author.

As applying, in some measure, to the text-books referred to, the following quotation is made from Professor Charles F. Richardson : " From the days when Alfred translated Boethius and Orosius instead of Cicero and Tacitus, wise teachers have used means toward ends, have taken simple books instead of (invariably) great ones, and have sought to stimulate as well as to instruct."

The histories to which reference is made are those in most common use. Their arrangement is partly according to value. Some of them contain little upon the earlier periods, and should be supplemented by cyclopedias and general works of reference. Green's and Gardiner's, the single-volume editions, are the most valuable ; while Curnow's, " written for English schools," is least so in some respects. Emery's *Notes* is a good guide to further study in literature. Where the histories afford no late information, as, for instance, in the case of Earl Rosebery, reference has been made to those periodicals most easily accessible to high schools and academies. To ensure completeness in this book as a practical manual, a carefully selected list of works for consultation has been placed at the end.

F. J. A.

MILFORD, N.H., Oct. 27, 1894.

ABBREVIATIONS.

———◦◦———

A.   = Anderson's *School History of England*[1] (Maynard, Merrill, & Co.).
M.   = Montgomery's *Leading Facts in English History* (Ginn & Co.).
B.   = Buckley's *History of England for Beginners* (Macmillan & Co.).
C.   = Curnow's *English History for Schools* (George Philip & Son).
T.   = Thalheimer's *History of England* (American Book Co.).
S.   = Stone's *History of England* (Thompson, Brown, & Co.).
D.   = Dickens' *Child's History of England* (American Book Co.).
G.   = Green's *Short History of the English People* (Harper & Brothers).
Gar.   = Gardiner's *Students' History of England* (Longmans, Green, & Co.).
E.   = Emery's *Notes on English Literature* (Ginn & Co.).
Br.   = Brooke's *Primer of English Literature* (American Book Co.).
Ap.   = Appendix.
Scrib.   = *Scribner's Monthly.*
Cent.   = *Century Magazine.*
Harper   = *Harper's Magazine.*
Forum   = *The Forum.*
R. of Rs. = *Review of Reviews.*

[1] Latest editions in all cases to 1894.

5

CONTENTS.

———◦◦——

ENGLISH SOVEREIGNS.

—•◦•—

SAXONS.

Egbert	827–839
Ethelwulf	839–858
Ethelbald	858–860
Ethelbert	860–866
Ethelred I.	866–871
Alfred	871–901
Edward the Elder . .	901–925
Athelstan	925–940
Edmund I.	940–946
Edred	946–955
Edwin	955–959
Edgar	959–975
Edward the Martyr . .	975–978
Ethelred II.	978–1016
Edmund II.	1016

DANES.

Canute I.	1017–1036
Harold I.	1036–1039
Canute II.	1039–1041

SAXONS RESTORED.

Edward the Confessor . .	1041–1066
Harold II.	1066

NORMANS.

William I.	1066–1087
William II.	1087–1100
Henry I.	1100–1135
Stephen	1135–1154

PLANTAGENETS.

Henry II.	1154–1189
Richard I.	1189–1199
John	1199–1216
Henry III.	1216–1272
Edward I.	1272–1307
Edward II.	1307–1327
Edward III.	1327–1377
Richard II.	1377–1399

LANCASTER.

Henry IV.	1399–1413
Henry V.	1413–1422
Henry VI.	1422–1461

YORK.

Edward IV.	1461–1483
Edward V.	1483
Richard III.	1483–1485

TUDORS.

Henry VII.	1485–1509
Henry VIII.	1509–1547
Edward VI.	1547–1553
Mary I. . . .	1553–1558
Elizabeth	1558–1603

STUARTS.

James I.	1603–1625
Charles I.	1625–1649
The Commonwealth . .	1649–1660
Charles II.	1660–1685
James II.	1685–1689
William and Mary . . .	1689–1702
Anne	1702–1714

HANOVERIANS.

George I.	1714–1727
George II.	1727–1760
George III.	1760–1820
George IV.	1820–1830
William IV.	1830–1837
Victoria	1837–

A TOPICAL OUTLINE OF ENGLISH HISTORY.

———oo⁚❂⁚oo———

PART I.—OLD ENGLAND.

—— 1066 A.D.

I. PREHISTORIC BRITAIN. —— 55 B.C.

1. Definitions, Area, Surface[1]: England, Ireland, Scotland, Wales.	A. 7, 8 ; M. 14–17 ; B. 3, 4 ; S. 1 ; D. 13.
2. The Island once a Part of the Continent ; Chalk-cliffs, Glaciers, Climate, Trees, and Animals.	M. 1, 2 ; T. 9 ; Gar. 1.
3. Rough-stone Age: Man of the River-drift and Cave ; Condition, Nature, Tools and Weapons, Duration, Remains.	M. 2–5 ; B. 4, 5 ; T. 9, 10 ; Gar. 1–3.
4. Polished-stone Age : a Higher Race ; Government, Mode of Life, Occupations, Arts, Burial.	M. 5–7 ; B. 5, 6 ; Gar. 3–5.
5. Bronze Age : The Celts ; Early Accounts, Dwellings, Tools and Weapons, Metals, Druidism.	A. 9, 10, 15–20 ; M. 7–11 ; B. 6, 7 ; C. 1, 2 ; T. 10 ; S. 1–5 ; D. 14–18 : Gar. 5–10.
What do we owe to Pre-historic Man?	

[1] See Preface.

11

II. Roman Britain.   55 B.C.–449 A.D.

1.ᐟ Condition of Europe.	M. 18; D. 18.
2. Cæsar; Invasions of Britain, 55 and 54 B.C.; Cassivelaunus.	A. 16, 17; M. 18–20; B. 7; C. 3, 4; T. 11; S. 6, 7; D. 19, 20; G. 5; Gar. 11, 12.
3. Invasion by Claudius, 43 A.D.; Caractacus, 50 A.D.	A. 20, 21; M. 20; B. 8; C. 5, 6; T. 12; S. 7; D. 20, 21; Gar. 13.
4. Fate of the Druids.	M. 21; B. 8; T. 12, 13; S. 7, 8; D. 22, 25.
5. Boadicea, 61.	A. 21, 22; M. 21, 22; B. 8; C. 6; T. 13, 14; S. 8; D. 22; Gar. 15.
6. Agricola, 78–84.	A. 22; M. 23; C. 6, 7; T. 14; S. 8; D. 23; G. 5; Gar. 16, 17.
7. Introduction of Christianity.	A. 26, 27; M. 22, 23; B. 9; C. 8; T. 17; S. 11; Gar. 23.
8. Departure of the Romans, 410–426 A.D.	A. 24; M. 27, 28; B. 9; C. 8, 9; T. 18; S. 11; D. 24; G. 6; Gar. 25, 26.
9. Roman Towns, Forts and Walls, Roads, Laws and Taxation.	A. 9, 22, 23, 25, 26; M. 12, 13, 21, 23–30; B. 8; C. 78; T. 14, 15, 17; S. 8–11; D. 24–26; G. 5, 6; Gar. 17–21.

III. Anglo-Saxon Britain.   449–1066.

1. The Teutons.	B. 10; C. 11; T. 16; G. 1, 2.
2. Saxon Pirates.	A. 31, 32; B. 10; C. 10, 12; T. 16; S. 12; D. 23; G. 7.
3. Picts and Scots; Vortigern.	A. 24, 25; M. 31, 32; B. 11; C. 10; T. 18; S. 12, 14; D. 27, 28; G. 6; Gar. 26.

14. Britain becomes England.	A. 34 ; M. 39, 40 ; C. 11, 12 ; T. 39 ; S. 14 ; D. 32 ; G. 44.
15. The Danish Invasion.	A. 40, 41 ; M. 40 ; B. 20 ; C. 20, 21 ; T. 26 ; S. 21 ; D. 38 ; G. 44–47 ; Gar. 56, 57.
16. Ethelwulf, 839–858 ; Ethelbald, 858–860 ; Ethelbert, 860–866 ; Ethelred I., 866–871.	A. 41–43 ; B. 21 ; C. 21, 22 ; T. 27 ; S. 21 ; D. 38 ; G. 46, 47 ; Gar. 57, 58.
17. Alfred the Great, 871–901.	A. 43–46 ; M. 40, 41 ; B. 21, 22 ; C. 22 ; T. 28, 29 ; S. 22, 23 ; D. 34–42 ; G. 47–52 ; Gar. 58–62.
18. Treaty of Wedmore, 878.	A. 45 ; M. 41, 42 ; B. 22 ; C. 22 ; T. 29 ; S. 23, 24 ; D. 37 ; G. 48 ; Gar. 59.
19. Alfred's Government, Laws, Navy, Literary Work.	A. 45–47 ; M. 42, 43 ; B. 23, 24 ; C. 23 ; T. 29–31 ; D. 37–42 ; G. 48–52 ; Gar. 60–62 ; E. 7 ; Br. 19, 20.
20. Edward the Elder, 901–925.	A. 47, 48 ; B. 24 ; C. 23, 24 ; T. 31 ; S. 24 ; D. 39 ; G. 53, 54 ; Gar. 62, 63.
21. Athelstan, 925–940 ; Edmund I., 940–946 ; Edred, 946–955 ; Edwin, 955–959.	A. 48–50 ; B. 24, 27 ; C. 24 ; T. 35–37 ; S. 24, 25 ; D. 43–48 ; G. 54–57 ; Gar. 63–67.
22. Dunstan and his Reforms.	A. 49, 52 ; M. 43, 44 ; B. 25–27 ; C. 24, 25 ; T. 36–39 ; S. 25, 26 ; D. 45–53 ; G. 55–61 ; Gar. 65–69.
23. Edgar the Peaceful, 959–975 ; Edward the Martyr, 975–978 ; Ethelred the Unready, 978–1016.	A. 50, 53 ; B. 27–29 ; C. 24, 25 ; T. 37–40 ; S. 26, 27 ; D. 48–53 ; G. 57–62 ; Gar. 67–69, 78–83.

24. Massacre of the Danes at the Festival of St. Brice, Nov. 13, 1002. | A. 53, 54; B. 29; C. 25, 26; T. 40; S. 27; D. 54; G. 62; Gar. 81.

25. Sweyn the Dane; **Edmund Ironside, 1016.** | A. 53–56; M. 44, 45; B. 29; C. 26; T. 40, 41; S. 27; D. 54–58; G. 62–65; Gar. 81–83.

26. The Danish Kings: **Canute the Great, 1017–1036; Harold Harefoot, 1036–1039; Hardicanute, 1039–1041.** | A. 56–60; M. 45; B. 29, 31; C. 27, 29; T. 42, 43; S. 28; D. 59–64; G. 65–67; Gar. 83–86.

27. **Edward the Confessor, 1041–1066.** | A. 60–64; M. 45, 46; B. 32–35; C. 30; T. 43–48; S. 29–32; D. 65–72; G. 68–70; Gar. 86–91.

28. Earl Godwin; **Harold II.** | A. 60–64; M. 46, 47; B. 32–35; C. 30–33; T. 43–48; S. 29–32; D. 65–78; G. 67–70; Gar. 87–96.

29. The Norwegian Invasion; Battle of Stamford Bridge, Sept. 25, 1066. | A. 64; M. 59; B. 36; C. 33; T. 49; S. 32; D. 73–75; G. 78, 79; Gar. 93–96.

SUPPLEMENTARY TOPICS ON ANGLO-SAXON BRITAIN.

1. Military Affairs (Alfred). | M. 54; Gar. 33, 60.

2. Feudal Tenure. | A. 86; M. 50–52; C. 15, 18; T. 54; S. 18; Gar. 69, 72.

3. Effects of Christianity on the Saxons. | M. 53, 54; B. 18; S. 18; G. 21–36; Gar. 49–51.

4. "Runes." | M. 54, 55.

5. The Anglo-Saxon Chronicle. | M. 55; B. 23; T. 54; G. 52; Gar. 61, 68; E. 7; Br. 21, 22.

6. Art and Architecture; Westminster Abbey. | A. 26, 34, 63, 67, 68; M. 46, 55, 56; B. 34, 73; C. 325; T. 23, 48, 52; S. 9, 16, 31; G. 144; Gar. 51, 91.

7. Industry and Commerce. | A. 68, 69; M. 56; B. 28; Gar. 38.

8. Life, Manners, and Customs. | A. 67, 68; M. 56, 57; S. 19, 20; Gar. 75–77.

PART II. — FEUDAL ENGLAND.

1066–1485.

I. The Norman Conquest. 1066–1154.

22. **Stephen,** 1135–1154.

A. 84 ; M. 75 ; B. 53 ; C. 59 ; S. 55 ; D. 114 ; G. 101 ; Gar. 131.

23. Matilda ; Battle of the Standard, 1138.

A. 83–85 ; M. 75, 76 ; B. 53, 54 ; C. 57, 61 ; T. 66–68 ; S. 55, 56 ; D. 107, 112–116 ; G. 100, 101 ; Gar. 132, 133.

24. Civil War ; Robber Barons.

A. 85 ; M. 76 ; B. 54, 55 ; C. 60, 62 ; T. 67, 68 ; S. 55, 56 ; D. 115–119 ; G. 101–103 ; Gar. 133–135.

25. Henry Plantagenet ; Treaty of Wallingford, 1153.

(End of the Saxon Chronicle.)

A. 85, 86 ; M. 77 ; B. 56 ; C. 62 ; T. 68, 69 ; D. 116, 117 ; G. 104 ; Gar. 136, 137.

SUPPLEMENTARY TOPICS ON THE NORMAN PERIOD.

1. Government : Kings, Councils, Courts of Justice, Trial by Battle, Land-Tenure, Taxes, "Tallies," Militia.

A. 91 ; M. 77–82 ; B. 50, 51 ; C. 58 ; T. 54 ; G. 83, 85, 96, 97 ; Gar. 112, 113, 126, 127.

2. Chivalry.

A. 88, 90 ; M. 83 ; B. 92 ; S. 68, 76, 77 ; G. 182, 183 ; Gar. 235.

3. The Church (Lanfranc and Anselm).

M. 82 ; B. 52 ; G. 85, 86, 89, 90, 103, 104 ; Gar. 88, 106–110, 128, 129.

4. Education ; Historical Works ; Bayeux Tapestry ; Effect of the Conquest on the English Language.

A. 92 ; M. 83, 84 ; B. 50, 51 ; C. 38, 106 ; S. 38, 75, 76 ; G. 117–121 ; Gar. 93–98 ; E. 7 ; Br. 22–28, 34.

5. Architecture.

M. 84, 85 ; Gar. 89.

6. Trade ; the Jews.

A. 102, 103, 116 ; M. 85, 118 ; B. 44 ; T. 75, 88, 89 ; S. 78 ; G. 86, 87 ; Gar. 115, 127, 128, 160.

7. Towns.

B. 51 ; G. 92–94.

8. Life, Manners, and Customs.

A. 91, 92 ; M. 85, 86 ; S. 78–80.

II. The Plantagenets. 1154-1399.

1. **Henry II.,** 1154-1189.	A. 95 ; M. 87 ; B. 56 ; C. 63 ; T. 70 ; S. 57 ; D. 120 ; G. 104 ; Gar. 138.
2. Possessions and Marriage.	M. 87 ; B. 57 ; S. 57 ; D. 120 ; G. 104, 106 ; Gar. 138.
3. Charter and Reforms.	A. 95 ; M. 88 ; B. 57 ; C. 64 ; T. 70 ; D. 120 ; G. 106, 109 ; Gar. 138-141.
4. Thomas à Becket.	A. 95-97 ; M. 89-93 ; B. 58-60 ; C. 64, 65 ; T. 70, 71 ; S. 58 ; D. 121-126 ; G. 103, 104, 106, 107 ; Gar. 140, 142-146.
5. Constitutions of Clarendon, 1164.	A. 97 ; M. 91 ; B. 59, 60 ; C. 65 ; T. 71 ; S. 58 ; D. 128 ; G. 107 ; Gar. 143-145.
6. Murder of Becket, Dec. 29, 1170; its Results.	A. 98 ; M. 93, 94 ; B. 60 ; C. 65 ; T. 72, 73 ; S. 58, 59 ; D. 127-136, 141 ; G. 108-110 ; Gar. 149-151.
7. **Henry,** Lord of Ireland.	A. 98-100 ; B. 60, 61 ; C. 66 ; T. 72, 73 ; D. 137-139 ; G. 445, 446 ; Gar. 151, 152.
8. End of Barons' Rebellion, 1074-1174.	A. 101 ; M. 95 ; C. 67 ; T. 74 ; G. 109, 110 ; Gar. 153, 154.
9. Circuits and Juries.	M. 95, 96 ; B. 58 ; C. 68 ; T. 74 ; S. 60 ; G. 109-112 ; Gar. 146-148.
10. Last Days of **Henry**; Results of Reign.	A. 100-102 ; M. 97 ; B. 62 ; C. 66-68 ; T. 74 ; S. 59 ; D. 139-146 ; G. 112 ; Gar. 155-158.

11. **Richard I.** (Lion-hearted), 1189–1199.

A. 102 ; M. 97, 98 ; B. 63 ; C. 69 ; T. 75 ; S. 61 ; D. 147 ; G. 112, 113 ; Gar. 159.

12. The Third Crusade ; Devices for raising Money ; Free Towns.

A. 103, 104 ; M. 99, 100–103 ; B. 63 ; C. 69, 72 ; T. 76 ; S. 61 ; D. 148–154 ; Gar. 159, 161, 169.

13. **Richard** in Germany ; his Death at Siege of Chaluz.

A. 104–106 ; M. 101 ; B. 64 ; C. 71 ; T. 77 ; S. 61 ; D. 154, 155, 157–159 ; G. 114, 115 ; Gar. 161, 162, 165.

14. **John Lackland,** 1199–1216.

A. 106 ; M. 103 ; B. 65 ; C. 73 ; T. 78 ; S. 62 ; D. 160 ; G. 122 ; Gar. 173.

15. The Loss of Normandy.

A. 107 ; M. 103, 104 ; B. 65, 66 ; C. 73 ; T. 78 ; S. 62 ; D. 160–166 ; Gar. 174, 176.

16. King against Church ; Stephen Langton.

A. 107, 108 ; M. 105 ; B. 66, 67 ; C. 74–76 ; T. 78, 79 ; S. 62 ; D. 167–171 ; G. 123–127 ; Gar. 176–181.

17. The Great Charter, June 15, 1215.

A. 108–110 ; M. 105–108 ; B. 67–69 ; C. 76, 77 ; T. 79–82 ; S. 62 ; D. 171–176 ; G. 127–130 ; Gar. 181–184.

18. Death of **John** ; Results of this Reign.

A. 110, 111 ; M. 108, 109 ; B. 69 ; C. 77 ; T. 81 ; S. 62 ; D. 176 ; G. 131 ; Gar. 185.

19. **Henry III.,** 1216–1272.

A. 111 ; M. 109 ; B. 71 ; C. 78 ; T. 83 ; S. 63 ; D. 177 ; G. 141 ; Gar. 185.

20. His Guardians and Advisers.

A. 111, 112 ; B. 71, 72 ; C. 78–80 ; T. 83 ; D. 177–183 ; G. 141, 142 ; Gar. 185–190.

21. Ratifications of the Great Charter.

A. 111, 112, 138 ; M. 109, 112 ; B. 74 ; C. 79, 82 ; T. 84 ; D. 179, 185 ; Gar. 185, 186.

33. Conquest of Scotland, 1296 ; Wallace and Bruce.

A. 116–120 ; M. 116, 117, 120 ; B. 83, 84, 86 ; C. 86, 87 ; T. 89, 93 ; S. 64, 65 ; D. 207–218 ; G. 184–193 ; Gar. 214–224.

34. **Edward II.** (Caernarvon), 1307–1327.

A. 121, 122 ; M. 121 ; B. 87 ; C. 88 ; T. 94 ; S. 65 ; D. 219 ; G. 207 ; Gar. 224.

35. Gaveston and the " Lords Ordainers," 1312.

A. 122 ; M. 122 ; B. 88 ; C. 90 ; T. 94 ; D. 219–224 ; G. 207–209 ; Gar. 224–226.

36. Bannockburn, June 24, 1314 ; Independence of Scotland, 1328.

A. 122, 123, 127 ; M. 122, 124 ; B. 88 ; C. 90, 94 ; T. 95 ; S. 65 ; D. 224–226 ; G. 211–216 ; Gar. 226–228.

37. Mortimer ; Deposition of the King.

A. 123–126 ; M. 123, 124 ; B. 89, 90 ; C. 91 ; T. 95 ; S. 65, 66 ; D. 226–232 ; G. 209–211 ; Gar. 228–231.

38. **Edward III.**, 1327–1377.

A. 126 ; M. 124 ; B. 90 ; C. 93 ; T. 95 ; S. 66 ; D. 233 ; G. 217 ; Gar. 231.

39. Beginning of the Hundred Years' War with France, 1337.

A. 128 ; M. 126, 127 ; B. 91, 92 ; C. 94, 95 ; T. 96 ; S. 66 ; D. 236–238 ; G. 223, 224 ; Gar. 232–240.

40. Battle of Crecy, Aug. 26, 1346 ; the Black Prince.

A. 128 ; M. 127–129 ; B. 92 ; C. 96, 97 ; T. 97 ; S. 67 ; D. 239–242 ; G. 225–227 ; Gar. 240–242.

41. Capture of Calais, 1347.

A. 129, 130 ; M. 129, 130 ; B. 93 ; C. 98 ; T. 97, 98 ; S. 67 ; D. 242–244 ; G. 228, 229 ; Gar. 242, 243.

42. Victory of Poitiers, Sept. 19, 1356.

A. 130–133 ; M. 130 ; B. 93 ; C. 99 ; T. 98 ; S. 67 ; D. 244–247 ; G. 229, 230 ; Gar. 251, 252.

43. Peace of Bretigny, 1360.

M. 130, 131 ; B. 93 ; C. 99 ; T. 99 ; D. 247 ; G. 231 ; Gar. 252–254.

44. The Black Death, 1349 (1361, 1369).

A. 130 ; M. 132, 133, 148 ; B. 95, 96 ; C. 98 ; T. 98 ; S. 68 ; D. 244 ; G. 247–250 ; Gar. 248–250.

45. Death of **Edward III.**

M. 134 ; B. 98 ; C. 100 ; T. 100, 101 ; S. 67, 68 ; D. 249, 250 ; G. 251 ; Gar. 262– 264.

46. **Richard II.,** 1377–1399.

A. 134 ; M. 134 ; B. 99 ; C. 101 ; T. 102 ; S. 69 ; D. 251 ; G. 255, 261 ; Gar. 266.

47. The Government during his Minority ; his Uncles.

A. 134, 144 ; M. 134, 141 ; B. 101, 102, 106 ; C. 101, 114 ; T. 102 ; S. 69 ; D. 251–256 ; G. 260, 261 ; Gar. 265.

48. Poll Tax and Peasant Revolt, 1381 ; Tyler and Ball.

A. 134–136 ; M. 135–137 ; B. 99, 100 ; C. 102, 103 ; T. 102, 103, 105 ; S. 69, 70 ; D. 256–265 ; G. 244–255 ; Gar. 267–269.

49. **Richard's** Misgovernment and Deposition.

A. 137 ; M. 139–141 ; B. 103, 104 ; C. 104, 105 ; T. 103, 104 ; S. 70 ; G. 262–264 ; Gar. 278–288.

SUPPLEMENTARY TOPICS ON THE PLANTAGENET PERIOD.

1. Separation of Lords and Commons, 1341.

M. 143 ; B. 95, 105 ; C. 84, 118 ; S. 74 ; G. 231–233 ; Gar. 243–246, 281.

2. Condition of Ireland.

A. 98, 99 ; B. 60, 61, 89, 97, 98 ; C. 66, 90, 91 ; T. 72–74 ; G. 444–448 ; Gar. 151, 152, 264, 265.

3. Arms and Armor; Scutage; Tournaments.

A. 90; M. 89, 98, 128, 129, 145, 146; B. 58, 62, 92; C. 64, 96, 97; S. 76, 77; G. 109; Gar. 141, 142, 235, 236, 241, 242.

4. The Wool Trade.

A. 133, 141; M. 125, 148; B. 94, 105; S. 78; D. 250; G. 224, 225; Gar. 210, 211, 237.

5. Towns; Fairs; Guilds.

A. 121; M. 99, 100, 142, 147; B. 63, 67, 72; S. 78; G. 129, 177-179, 193-204; Gar. 168-170, 183, 240.

6. Architecture.

M. 110, 147; S. 71-73; G. 202; Gar. 170, 171, 206, 207, 246-248.

7. Education: Cambridge, 1257; Oxford, 1264.

A. 142; M. 102, 146; T. 86; S. 17, 69, 74-76; G. 217-219; Gar. 167, 168, 207, 258; Br. 22-24.

8. Friars; Roger Bacon.

A. 121, 141; M. 111, 144; B. 73; T. 86, 87; S. 73, 75; G. 138-141, 147-152; Gar. 190-192; E. 8; Br. 26, 27, 35.

9. Life, Manners, and Customs.

A. 139-141; M. 98, 148, 149; B. 72; C. 108-112; S. 74, 78-80; G. 244-247; Gar. 248-250, 268, 272-277, 281; E. 10; Br. 37, 38.

LITERATURE OF THE AGE OF CHAUCER.

1. Sir John Mandeville, 1300-1372;
Voyages and Travels.

A. 133; M. 133, 147; S. 69; Br. 49; E. 11.

2. John Wycliffe, 1324-1384;
Translation of the Bible.

A. 133, 138, 142; M. 138, 139, 144; B. 96, 97, 105; C. 108; S. 70; D. 250; G. 235-244, 258-260; Gar. 261, 266; E. 12, 13; Br. 40, 41.

3. William Langland, 1332(?)-1400;
Vision of Piers Ploughman.

M. 133; B. 96; T. 107; G. 255-258; Gar. 258, 259; E. 10, 11; Br. 36-40.

4. Geoffrey Chaucer, 1340(?)-1400;
The Canterbury Tales.

A. 138, 142; M. 137; B. 96; C. 106, 107; T. 105, 106; S. 70, 71; G. 219-223; Gar. 270-272; E. 14, 15; Br. 22-49.

III. Lancaster and York. 1399–1485.

1. **Henry IV.** (Lancaster), 1399–1413.	A. 146; M. 150; B. 107; C. 113; T. 108; S. 81; D. 266; G. 265; Gar. 286, 287, 289.
2. Conspiracies against him.	A. 146, 147; M. 151, 152; B. 107, 108; C. 115–117; T. 108, 109; S. 81; D. 266–272; G. 265, 266; Gar. 292–295.
3. Persecution of the Lollards; the First Martyr, 1401.	A. 146; M. 153; B. 109, 110; C. 118, 119; T. 108; S. 81; D. 266; G. 265; Gar. 291, 292.
4. Battle of Shrewsbury, July 23, 1403.	A. 147; M. 152, 153; B. 108; C. 117; T. 109; S. 81; D. 270, 271; G. 266; Gar. 293, 294.
5. The King's Last Days.	A. 148; M. 154; B. 110; C. 119; T. 110; S. 82; D. 272, 273; G. 266; Gar. 298, 299.
6. **Henry V.**, 1413–1422.	A. 148; M. 155; B. 110; C. 120; T. 110; S. 82; D. 274; G. 266; Gar. 297.
7. Revolt of the Lollards.	A. 149; M. 155; B. 112; C. 121; T. 110; S. 82; D. 274, 275; G. 266, 267; Gar. 297, 298.
8. Reasons for Renewing War with France.	A. 149; M. 155, 156; B. 112; C. 122; T. 111; S. 83; D. 275, 277; G. 267; Gar. 300, 301.
9. Battle of Agincourt, Oct. 25, 1415.	A. 149; M. 156, 157; B. 113; C. 122–124; T. 111, 112; S. 83, 84; D. 277–283; G. 268, 269; Gar. 301–303.

10. Treaty of Troyes, 1420; Results.	A. 149, 150; M. 157, 158; B. 113, 114; C. 124, 125; T. 112, 113; S. 84; D. 284–288; G. 270; Gar. 304–306.
11. **Henry VI.**, 1422–1461.	A. 151; M. 158; B. 114; C. 126; T. 114; S. 84; D.[1] 9; G. 271; Gar. 307.
12. Siege of Orleans, 1428–1429.	A. 151, 152; M. 158; B. 114, 115; C. 127, 128; T. 114, 115; S. 84, 85; D. 9–11; G. 275–278; Gar. 309, 310.
13. Joan of Arc.	A. 152, 153; M. 159; B. 115; C. 128, 129; T. 115; S. 84, 85; D. 12–22; G. 274–279; Gar. 310–312.
14. End of the Hundred Years' War, 1453.	A. 153; M. 159; B. 116; C. 131; T. 115; D. 23; G. 279–281; Gar. 312–320.
15. Margaret of Anjou, 1445.	A. 153, 154; M. 159, 160; B. 116; C. 129; T. 116; S. 85; D. 24, 25; G. 280, 283, 285, 287, 288; Gar. 317.
16. Troubles at Home.	A. 154, 155; M. 160, 161; B. 116, 117; C. 130; T. 116, 117; S. 86; D. 23–26; G. 281–283; Gar. 320–324.
17. Jack Cade's Rebellion, 1450.	A. 154; M. 161; B. 118; C. 130, 131; T. 117; S. 86; D. 26–29; G. 281, 282; Gar. 322, 323.
18. Wars of the Roses, 1455–1485.	A. 155; M. 162–164; B. 118, 119; C. 131; T. 118; S. 86; D. 30; G. 283; Gar. 324.

[1] Vol. II.

19. Battle of St. Albans, May 22, 1455; Northampton, July 10, 1460; Warwick, the "King-Maker."

A. 155, 156; M. 165; B. 118, 119; C. 131, 132; T. 118; S. 86; D. 30–32; G. 282, 283, 286–288; Gar. 324–327, 332–334.

20. Battle of Wakefield, Dec. 29, 1460.

A. 156; M. 165; B. 119; C. 132, 133; T. 118; S. 86; D. 33, 34; G. 284; Gar. 327, 328.

21. Edward IV. (York), 1461–1483.

A. 157; M. 167; B. 120; C. 134; T. 120; S. 87; D. 35, 36; G. 285, 292; Gar. 329.

22. Battle of Towton, March 29, 1461.

A. 157; M. 166; B. 120; C. 134; T. 120; S. 87; D. 36; G. 285; Gar. 328, 329.

23. Continuation of the War.

A. 157, 158; M. 167; B. 120, 121; C. 135–137; T. 120, 121; S. 88; D. 36–42; G. 286, 287; Gar. 331–334.

24. Barnet and Tewkesbury, 1471.

A. 158, 159; M. 167; B. 122; C. 137; T. 121; S. 88; D. 42–44; G. 288; Gar. 334.

25. Edward's "Benevolences."

M. 168, 169; B. 122, 123; C. 142; D. 44–46; G. 290, 293; Gar. 335.

26. Edward V., April 9–June 26, 1483.

A. 160; M. 169; B. 124; C. 140; T. 122; S. 89; D. 47; G. 299; Gar. 337.

27. Gloucester Protector; Rivers, Grey, Hastings, and the Princes murdered.

A. 160, 161; M. 169, 170; B. 124–126; C. 141; T. 122, 123; S. 89; D. 47–56; G. 299; Gar. 337–340, 342.

28. Richard III., 1483–1485.

A. 161, 163; M. 170; B. 126; C. 141; T. 123; S. 89; D. 54; G. 299; Gar. 341.

29. Henry Tudor.

A. 141 ; M. 171, 172 ; B. 127 ; C. 142, 143 ; T. 123 ; S. 89 ; D. 56, 57 ; G. 299–303 ; Gar. 341, 342.

30. Bosworth Field, Aug. 22, 1485.

A. 162, 163 ; M. 172, 173 ; B. 128 ; C. 143 ; T. 124 ; S. 89, 90 ; D. 58–60 ; G. 300, 301 ; Gar. 343.

31. End of the Wars of the Roses ; their Effects.

A. 155, 163–165 ; M. 173, 174 ; B. 128, 129 ; T. 124 ; S. 90, 91 ; G. 288–290, 301 ; Gar. 330, 343, 345.

SUPPLEMENTARY TOPICS ON THE LANCASTER AND YORK PERIOD.

1. Parliament.

M. 175; B. 123; C. 118, 135, 136; G. 264, 265, 271–274, 289–293; Gar. 329, 330.

2. Agriculture and Trade.

A. 165; M. 178; B. 122; S. 90; G. 292, 293.

3. Architecture.

A. 168; M. 177, 178; Gar. 358.

4. William Caxton; the Printing Press, 1474.

A. 160, 166; M. 167, 168, 177; B. 123, 124; C. 138, 139; T. 121, 122; S. 89; G. 295–299; Gar. 358; E. 17, 18; Br. 54, 55.

5. Learning and Literature : Sir Thomas Malory, *Morte D'Arthur;* the Drama.

A. 166, 167; M. 177; C. 139; S. 91; G. 274, 294–299, 427; E. 16–18, 31, 32; Br. 50–56, 90–92.

6. Life, Manners, and Customs.

A. 164; M. 178; B. 122; S. 91; G. 288–292; Gar. 320–322, 330, 331.

7. End of Feudal England (or Middle Ages).

B. 128, 129; C. 145; T. 124; G. 301.

PART III. — MODERN ENGLAND.

1485 ——.

I. The Tudors. 1485–1603.

1. **Henry VII.**, 1485–1509.	A. 171; M. 179; B. 131; C. 145; T. 127; S. 97; D. 61; G. 301; Gar. 343.
2. Power of the King; Growth of Nationality.	A. 171, 174, 175, 208; M. 180, 181, 184, 224; B. 134, 147; C. 155, 156; T. 127; S. 99; D. 61; G. 301, 302; Gar. 345, 346, 349, 356–358.
3. "The Star Chamber;" Empson and Dudley.	A. 174–176, 228; M. 182, 183; B. 132–134; C. 156, 157; T. 131; S. 98, 100; D. 74, 77; G. 302, 303; Gar. 348, 349, 357, 363.
4. Symnel and Warbeck.	A. 171–174; M. 184; B. 131–133; C. 147, 148, 151–155; T. 129, 130; S. 97, 98; D. 62–72; G. 301; Gar. 346, 347.
5. **Henry's** Politic Marriages.	M. 184; B. 134, 135; C. 157, 158; T. 130; S. 100; D. 73; G. 311; Gar. 354, 356.
6. Columbus; Vasco de Gama; Cabot.	A. 175; M. 185, 186; B. 135; C. 158; T. 128; S. 99, 100; D. 75; G. 303, 395, 506; Gar. 354, 356.

29

7. **Henry VIII.**, 1509–1547.

A. 175; M. 187; B. 136; C. 159; T. 132; S. 101; D. 76; G. 308; Gar. 361.

8. The New Learning: Colet; Erasmus; More, *Utopia*.

A. 182, 184, 214; M. 188, 189, 197, 216; B. 135, 136, 142, 150; C. 168, 200, 201; T. 128, 136–138; S. 104–106; D. 91, 93–95; G. 303–323, 325, 327, 333, 339, 340, 342–344; Gar. 366–368, 371, 387, 388, 392, 394; E. 17, 20; Br. 56–58.

9. Martin Luther (the German Reformation).

A. 174, 179; M. 189, 190; B. 136, 143; C. 168, 169; T. 136, 137; S. 102, 103; D. 85, 86, 91; G. 320–322, 354; Gar. 377, 379, 387, 388, 396.

10. Flodden Field, Sept. 9, 1513.

A. 177; M. 190; B. 137; C. 162; T. 133; S. 102; D. 79; G. 380; Gar. 364.

11. "Field of the Cloth of Gold," 1520.

A. 178; M. 190; B. 139; C. 164; T. 134, 135; S. 102; D. 82–84; G. 324; Gar. 369.

12. Catharine of Aragon; Anne Boleyn.

A. 176, 180–185; M. 190–194; B. 136, 139–141; C. 160, 167; T. 135–138, 140; S. 103–105; D. 76, 78, 80, 86–89, 91–93, 97–99; G. 311, 328–330, 336, 337, 348; Gar. 379–390, 392, 395.

13. Cardinal Wolsey; Thomas Cromwell.

A. 177–182, 186; M. 191–193, 198; B. 138–140; C. 163, 164; T. 133–137, 140; S. 103–105; D. 81–87, 89–91, 95, 102, 103; G. 310, 322–

21. Book of Common Prayer, 1549; Thomas Cranmer.

A. 189, 191, 194, 196; M. 193, 202; B. 141, 148, 151, 154; C. 174, 175, 177, 178, 184, 186; T. 137, 138, 143, 148; S. 101, 104, 106, 108; D. 108, 110, 115–117, 122; G. 334, 337, 356, 358–360, 362, 367, 368; Gar. 389, 400, 409, 413–416, 418, 425, 426; Br. 59.

22. Seizure of Lands; Rents; Bishop Latimer.

A. 189, 191, 196; M. 201, 202; B. 148, 149, 151, 154; C. 184; T. 148; S. 108; D. 111, 122; G. 326, 327, 352, 356, 360, 362, 366, 367; Gar. 390, 417, 425; E. 21; Br. 59.

23. Lady Jane Grey named as Successor.

A. 192; M. 204; B. 150; C. 178; T. 145; S. 107; D. 116; G. 361; Gar. 420.

24. **Mary I.,** 1553–1558.

A. 193; M. 205; B. 150; C. 179; T. 146; S. 107; D. 118; G. 361; Gar. 421.

25. Wyatt's Rebellion, 1554.

A. 194; M. 205; B. 152, 153; C. 180, 181; T. 147; D. 123, 124; G. 362, 363; Gar. 423.

26. Execution of Lady Jane Grey, 1554.

A. 193–195; M. 205, 206; B. 150–153; C. 179–182; T. 145–147; S. 107, 108; D. 118–120, 122, 124, 125; G. 363; Gar. 423.

27. Marriage of **Mary** to Philip II. of Spain, 1554.

A. 194; M. 205, 206; B. 152, 153; C. 183; T. 146, 147, 148, 149; S. 107; D. 122, 123, 127; G. 362, 363, 368; Gar. 421, 423.

28. Efforts to restore Catholicism; Cardinal Pole.

A. 194–197; M. 206, 207; B. 151, 153, 154; C. 183, 184; T. 146–149; S. 108; D. 121–123, 127–135; G. 362–368, 370; Gar. 421–427.

29. Death of **Mary.**

A. 197; M. 207, 208; B. 152, 155; C. 184; T. 149; S. 109; D. 134; G. 369; Gar. 427.

30. Martyrs.

A. 195, 196; M. 207, 208; B. 154; C. 184; T. 147–149; S. 108; D. 128–135; G. 361–368; Gar. 424–427; E. 21.

31. **Elizabeth,** 1558–1603 (A Reign of Internal Development).

A. 198; M. 208; B. 155; C. 185; T. 151; S. 109; D. 136; G. 369; Gar. 428; E. 23.

32. Her Counsellors; Sir William Cecil.

A. 198, 199; M. 210; B. 157; C. 186, 192; T. 151; S. 112; D. 137; G. 371, 373, 376, 378, 381, 389–392, 396; Gar. 429, 433, 441, 479, 480.

33. Religious Parties:
Catholics,
Jesuits;
Protestants,
Puritans.

A. 199; M. 209; B. 157–159, 169; C. 189, 190; T. 155; S. 109, 110, 115; D. 152, 155, 156; G. 369, 376–379, 382–386, 388–392, 401, 405–410, 460–474; Gar. 396, 428–437, 443–446, 453–456, 468, 470.

34. Religious Legislation: Acts of Supremacy and Uniformity, 1559; Thirty-nine Articles, 1563; Court of High Commission, 1583.

A. 209; M. 210–212; B. 157, 161; C. 185, 186, 189; T. 151, 152; S. 110; D. 137, 138, 151; G. 377, 379, 384, 385, 406; Gar. 419, 420, 429, 430, 454, 468, 470, 472.

35. Question of the Queen's Marriage.

A. 199 ; M. 213 ; B. 161 ; C. 187 ; T. 152 ; S. 109; D. 142,154, 155 ; G. 375, 381, 384, 387, 414 ; Gar. 431, 432, 435, 443, 444, 446.

36. Mary, Queen of Scots.

A. 201–203, 215 ; M. 209, 218 ; B. 159, 161, 162 ; C. 186, 187 ; T. 153, 154 ; S. 110 ; D. 138–146 ; G. 369, 370, 375, 379–388 ; Gar. 432–440.

37. Her Imprisonment and Execution by **Elizabeth,** 1568–1587.

A. 203–205 ; M. 218, 219 ; B. 163, 164, 167 ; C. 182, 188, 190, 192, 193 ; T. 154–156 ; S. 111 ; D. 146–151, 157–161 ; G. 388–392, 416, 417 ; Gar. 440–446, 456–458.

38. The Netherlands and William of Orange.

A. 201, 205, 212 ; M. 219 ; B. 157, 160, 164–166 ; C. 190, 191 ; T. 155 ; D. 152, 156 ; G. 375, 388–390, 411–416 ; Gar. 443–445, 449, 450, 453–457.

39. The Spanish Armada, July, 1588.

A. 201 ; M. 220–222 ; B. 168, 169 ; C. 195, 196 ; T. 155, 157, 158 ; S. 111, 112 ; D. 162–164 ; G. 375, 417–420 ; Gar. 446, 447, 458–463.

40. Sir Walter Raleigh.

A. 200, 214, 220–222 ; M. 214, 217, 236, 237 ; B. 169, 170, 181 ; C. 197, 202, 206, 211, 212, 351 ; T. 162, 163 ; S. 112, 116, 122, 123 ; D. 164, 167 ; G. 399, 488, 489, 506 ; Gar. 463, 464, 481, 486, 489; E. 27, 28 ; Br. 110.

41. Sir Martin Frobisher ; Sir Francis Drake.

A. 200, 211 ; M. 217, 220 ; B. 160, 169 ; C. 194, 195 ; T. 155 ; S. 112, 114 ; D. 162, 163 ; G. 415, 416, 421, 506 ; Gar. 448–451, 457, 458, 460, 464.

42. The Irish Rebellion, 1595–1602.

A. 206 ; M. 222 ; B. 171 ; C. 198, 199 ; T. 158, 159 ; S. 112 ; D. 165 ; G. 455–458 ; Gar. 451–453, 475–478.

43. **Elizabeth's** Last Days ; Splendor of her Reign.

A. 199, 200, 206–208, 210, 212, 214 ; M. 215–217, 222, 223 ; B. 159, 163, 169–172 ; C. 199 ; T. 156, 157, 159, 160 ; S. 109, 110, 113, 114 ; D. 165–169 ; G. 374, 393–401, 458, 459 ; Gar. 464, 479, 480.

SUPPLEMENTARY TOPICS ON THE TUDOR PERIOD.

1. The Church of England, 1559.

A. 183; M. 224, 225; B. 154; C. 175, 185, 186, 189; T. 151: S. 109, 115; G. 460; Gar. 396, 429, 472; E. 17; Br. 58, 59.

2. East India Company, 1600.

A. 221; M. 217; B. 169; C. 311; T. 164; S. 115; G. 396; Gar. 758.

3. Trade ; "Monopolies."

A. 210–212; M. 215, 224, 227; B. 160, 172; C. 194, 215; T. 129, 156, 157; S. 116; D. 169; G. 394–396, 402, 405; Gar. 464, 476, 478.

4. First Poor Law, 1601.

M. 222 ; B. 159 ; G. 374, 392, 393 ; Gar. 911.

5. Grammar Schools.

M. 225; B. 150; S. 121; G. 398, 407, 421; Gar. 419.

6. Architecture.

M. 226; S. 118; G. 396, 397; Gar. 465, 467, 469, 471.

7. Life, Manners, and Customs.

A. 210, 213, 214; M. 227, 228; B. 160, 161; S. 118-121; D. 169; G. 396-401; Gar. 464-468.

ELIZABETHAN LITERATURE (THE GOLDEN AGE).

1. Sir Philip Sidney, 1554-1586; *Arcadia.*

A. 205, 208; M. 217; B. 170; C. 191, 201; D. 156; G. 400, 416, 422; Gar. 457; E. 25, 26; Br. 71-78.

2. Edmund Spenser, 1552-1599; *The Faerie Queen.*

A. 208; M. 215, 218; B. 170; C. 202, 203; T. 160; S. 110; D. 169; G. 370, 374, 420-426; Gar. 473; E. 24, 25; Br. 80-84.

3. Shakespeare, 1564-1616; *Dramas.*

A. 208, 215, 216; M. 215, 218, 226, 302; B. 65, 170; C. 203; T. 160; S. 110, 127, 128; D. 169; G. 398, 400, 426-436; Gar. 474; E. 32-36; Br. 92-103.

4. Ben Jonson, 1574-1637; *Dramas.*

A. 208, 289; M. 218; C. 288; S. 127; G. 437; E. 36; Br. 103, 104.

5. Francis Bacon, 1561-1626; *Essays.*

A. 208, 223; M. 218, 236; B. 170, 183; C. 188, 202, 212; T. 160, 166; S. 110, 125; D. 169; G. 438-442, 477, 490, 491; Gar. 474, 475, 486, 495, 496; E. 29, 30; Br. 109.

II. The Stuarts (and the Commonwealth). 1603-1714.

1. **James I.**, 1603-1625.   A. 219 ; M. 229 ; B. 175 ; C. 205 ; T. 162 ; S. 122 ; D. 170 ; G. 386, 388, 474 ; Gar. 481.

2. " Divine Right of Kings."   A. 219 ; M. 232 ; B. 176 ; C. 206 ; T. 163 ; S. 126, 127, 157 ; D. 171 ; G. 477-479 ; Gar. 492, 619 ; Br. 132, 133.

3. Hampton Court Conference, Jan. 14, 1604 ; Translation of the Bible, 1611.   A. 225 ; M. 230-232 ; B. 177, 178 ; C. 207 ; T. 163, 164 ; S. 124 ; G. 460-462, 480 ; Gar. 481, 482.

4. The Gunpowder Plot, 1605.   A. 220 ; M. 232, 233 ; B. 178, 179 ; C. 208 ; T. 162, 163 ; S. 123, 124 ; D. 174-182 ; G. 482, 483 ; Gar. 483.

5. American Colonies ; the " Pilgrim Fathers," 1620.   A. 221, 225, 282 ; M. 233-235 ; B. 178 ; C. 351-356 ; T. 163-165 ; S. 124, 125 ; G. 472, 473, 505-514 ; Gar. 489.

6. King and Commons.   A. 223 ; M. 235, 236 ; B. 178-180, 182-184 ; C. 214, 215 ; T. 165, 166 ; S. 126 ; D. 183, 184 ; G. 480-486, 489-495 ; Gar. 482-487, 490-496, 500, 501.

7. **Charles I.**, 1625-1649.   A. 225 ; M. 238 ; B. 185 ; C. 216 ; T. 169 ; S. 128 ; D. 193 ; G. 496 ; Gar. 502.

8. Schemes for Raising Money ; John Hampden.   A. 226, 237 ; M. 238-241 ; B. 186-188, 193, 198 ; C. 217, 218, 221, 222, 228 ; T. 169-172 ; S. 128 ; D. 194, 195, 201, 203, 207, 208, 210, 218 ; G. 496, 497, 499-501, 516-518, 527-531, 538, 550 ; Gar. 502-515, 523, 524.

9. The Petition of Right, 1628.	A. 227; M. 239; B. 189; C. 219; T. 170; S. 129; D. 196; G. 501–503, 519; Gar. 508–510.
10. The Presbyterians.	A. 241, 250, 252, 270, 281; M. 241; B. 177; C. 223; G. 468–472, 523, 543, 544, 686, 812, 813; Gar. 430, 431, 434, 470, 532, 543, 546, 551–556, 583–586, 599.
11. The Scotch Covenanters, 1638.	A. 229, 230; M. 241; B. 193, 194; C. 223; T. 172; S. 130; D. 202–204; G. 522–525, 529–534; Gar. 524–527, 529.
12. Long Parliament, 1640–1660.	A. 230–237; M. 241–243; B. 194–197; C. 223–226; T. 173–181; S. 131; D. 204–227; G. 534–571; Gar. 529–557.
13. The Civil War; Cavaliers and Roundheads.	A. 232–237, 281; M. 243, 244; B. 197, 198; C. 226, 227; T. 174–176; S. 132, 133; D. 213–221; G. 542–559; Gar. 534–552.
14. Oliver Cromwell; his " Ironsides."	A. 239; M. 244, 245; B. 199; C. 228–230; T. 177; S. 133, 135; D. 202, 216, 218, 221; G. 466, 467, 552–557, 562; Gar. 539, 540, 545.
15. Marston Moor, July 2, 1644; Naseby, June 14, 1645.	A. 238, 239; M. 245; B. 199, 200; C. 228–230; T. 178; S. 135, 136; D. 218, 219; G. 552, 553, 557, 558; Gar. 542–544, 548.

16. King and Army.

A. 240, 241 ; M. 245, 246 ; B. 200, 201 ; C. 230 ; T. 178, 179 ; D. 220–227 ; G. 559–571 ; Gar. 553–557.

17. " Pride's Purge," 1648.

A. 241 ; M. 246 ; B. 201 ; C. 231 ; T. 180 ; D. 227 ; G. 571 ; Gar. 557.

18. Trial and Execution of Charles I., Jan. 30, 1649.

A. 242, 243 ; M. 246, 247 ; B. 202 ; C. 231 ; T. 180–182 ; S. 137–139 ; D. 228–232 ; G. 571, 572 ; Gar. 557–560.

19. Establishment of the Commonwealth, 1649–1660.

A. 243 ; M. 247, 248 ; B. 202 ; C. 232 ; T. 183 ; S. 141 ; D. 233 ; G. 572 ; Gar. 561.

20. Difficulties of the New Republic.

M. 248 ; B. 203 ; C. 233 ; D. 233, 234 ; G. 572–574 ; Gar. 561, 562.

21. Prince Charles ; Ireland, Drogheda, Sept. 11, 1649 ; Scotland, Worcester, Sept. 3, 1651.

A. 244, 245 ; M. 249 ; B. 203–206 ; C. 233–235 ; T. 183–185 ; S. 142–144 ; D. 234–241 ; G. 574–578 ; Gar. 562–564.

22. Navigation Act, 1651 ; Dutch War, 1652–1654.

A. 246 ; M. 253, 254 ; B. 206, 207 ; C. 235, 236 ; T. 185 ; S. 144, 145 ; D. 241, 242 ; G. 579, 580 ; Gar. 564, 565.

23. Cromwell and Parliament.

A. 246, 247 ; M. 249, 250 ; B. 207, 208 ; C. 237, 238 ; T. 186 ; S. 145, 146 ; D. 242, 243 ; G. 578–584 ; Gar. 565–568.

24. Cromwell as Protector, 1653–1658.

A. 247–249 ; M. 250–253 ; B. 208–211 ; C. 238, 239 ; T. 187–189 ; S. 146, 147 ; D. 243–251 ; G. 584–596 ; Gar. 568–574.

25. His Death.

A. 249; M. 254, 255; B. 211, 212; C. 240; T. 189; S. 147, 148; D. 252, 253; G. 596-598; Gar. 574, 575.

26. Richard Cromwell, Sept. 3, 1658–April 22, 1659.

A. 250; M. 255-257; B. 212; C. 240, 241; T. 189; S. 148; D. 253; G. 598, 599; Gar. 574.

27. **Charles II.**, 1660-1685.

A. 250; M. 257; B. 213, 214; C. 242; T. 189-191; S. 149; D. 253-256; G. 600, 605; Gar. 575, 576, 578.

28. Punishment of the Regicides.

A. 252; M. 260; C. 243; D. 257; G. 617, 618; Gar. 580.

29. Corporation Act, 1661 ; Act of Uniformity, 1662.

A. 252; M. 260, 261; B. 217; C. 243, 245; T. 192; S. 150; D. 258, 259, 261; G. 621-623; Gar. 585.

30. New Amsterdam ; Renewal of the Dutch War, 1664-1667.

A. 254; M. 262, 264, 265; B. 219-221; C. 245, 246; T. 193; D. 262, 265, 267; G. 628, 635, 640, 646.

31. The Plague, 1665; the Great Fire, 1666.

A. 254, 255; M. 262, 263; B. 219-221; C. 246, 247; T. 193; S. 150; D. 262-267; G. 628, 629; Gar. 590, 592.

32. The "Cabal," 1667.

A. 256; M. 258, 259; B. 221-223; C. 249, 250; T. 194; S. 150; D. 268; G. 636, 639, 653, 654; Gar. 602, 608, 611.

33. Treaty of Dover, 1670.

A. 257; M. 264, 265; B. 222-224; C. 250, 251; T. 194, 195; G. 637-639; Gar. 600, 601.

34. The Popish Plot, 1678.
A. 258, 259; M. 266, 270; B. 224; C. 253–255, 260; T. 195–197, 200; S. 151; D. 272–274, 287; G. 649–652, 656, 691; Gar. 615, 616.

35. Habeas Corpus Act, 1679.
A. 259; M. 269; B. 225; C. 256; S. 151; G. 662; Gar. 617.

36. Whigs and Tories; the Rye House Plot, 1683.
A. 259; M. 266–268; B. 226, 227; C. 256–258; T. 196, 197; S. 151; G. 657, 661; Gar. 620–626.

37. Death of **Charles II.**
A. 261; M. 269, 270; B. 228; C. 258; T. 198, 199; D. 284, 285; G. 663, 664; Gar. 627.

38. **James II.**, 1685–1689.
A. 262; M. 270; B. 228; C. 259; T. 200; S. 152; D. 286; G. 664; Gar. 634.

39. Monmouth's Rebellion; Sedgemoor, July 6, 1685.
A. 262, 263; M. 271, 272; B. 226, 230, 231; C. 263, 264; T. 197, 200, 201; S. 152; D. 284, 287–291; G. 630, 655, 657, 661, 664, 665; Gar. 620, 635.

40. The Bloody Assizes; Jeffreys and Kirke.
A. 263, 265; M. 272–274; B. 232, 239; C. 264, 265; T. 201; S. 152; D. 280, 281, 283, 291–295, 302; G. 665, 666, 672; Gar. 625, 635, 637, 638.

41. Declaration of Indulgence, April 4, 1687; Oxford.
A. 265; M. 274–276; B. 235; C. 267, 268; T. 201, 202; D. 295–297; G. 667, 671; Gar. 640, 641.

42. Trial of the Seven Bishops, June 29 and 30, 1688.
A. 265; M. 276, 277; B. 237, 238; C. 268–271; T. 202; S. 152; D. 297–299; G. 671, 672; Gar. 642, 643.

43. William of Orange invited to the Throne ; the Revolution of 1688.

A. 266; M. 277–280; B. 238, 239 ; C. 271–273; T. 198, 202, 203 ; S. 152, 153 ; D. 268–270, 299–304; G. 640, 647, 649, 655, 658, 672–683 ; Gar. 589, 605, 609, 613, 643–648.

44. Convention Parliament, Jan. 22, 1689 ; Declaration of Rights.

A. 267 ; M. 280 ; B. 239, 240 ; C. 272 ; T. 203 ; S. 153 ; G. 682, 683 ; Gar. 646, 647.

45. **William and Mary** (Orange-Stuart), 1689–1702.

A. 269 ; M. 280 ; B. 240; C. 272 ; T. 207 ; S. 153 ; D. 305 ; G. 683 ; Gar. 649.

46. Jacobites and Nonjurors.

A. 269, 274 ; M. 281 ; B. 241 ; C. 297 ; S. 153 ; G. 690–692, 694–696 ; Gar. 651, 652, 664–666.

47. Mutiny and Toleration Acts, 1689.

A. 269, 270 ; M. 281, 282 ; B. 244 ; C. 274 ; G. 689, 690 ; Gar. 649–652.

48. The Bill of Rights, 1689.

A. 267 ; M. 282, 283 ; B. 240 ; C. 274 ; T. 204 ; S. 153 ; G. 688 ; Gar. 656.

49. Revolt in Ireland; Act of Attainder ; Battle of the Boyne, July 1, 1690.

A. 271, 272 ; M. 285, 286 ; B. 242–245 ; C. 274–277 ; T. 208 ; G. 686–688, 692–694 ; Gar. 654–657.

50. Revolt in Scotland ; Massacre of Glencoe, Feb. 13, 1692.

A. 270 ; M. 287 ; B. 241, 242 ; C. 275, 276 ; T. 207, 208 ; G. 685, 686 ; Gar. 652–654.

51. Continental Wars ; Peace of Ryswick, Sept. 11, 1697.

A. 272–274 ; M. 287 ; B. 245, 246, 251 ; C. 277–279 ; T. 209, 210 ; S. 154 ; G. 684–696, 699–701 ; Gar. 657, 658, 663, 667.

52. The National Debt and the Bank of England, 1694.	A. 275; M. 288; B. 247, 248, 257; C. 278; S. 154; G. 699; Gar. 658–660.
53. Act of Settlement, 1701.	A. 278; M. 283, 300; B. 253; C. 279; T. 203, 212; G. 705; Gar. 672–674.
54. Death of **William**; Results of his Reign.	A. 274, 275; M. 288, 289; B. 253; C. 280; T. 211; S. 154; D. 305; G. 703, 704, 707; Gar. 647, 648, 676.
55. **Anne**, 1702–1714.	A. 275; M. 289; B. 254; C. 281; T. 212; S. 155; D. 306; G. 707; Gar. 676.
56. Whigs and Tories; High Church and Low Church.	M. 290, 291; B. 254; C. 281; S. 151; G. 570, 675, 690, 691; Gar. 620.
57. War of the Spanish Succession, 1702–1713.	A. 276, 277; M. 291–293; B. 254–257; C. 280–285; T. 210, 211, 213, 214; S. 155; G. 701–719; Gar. 667–672, 674, 675, 678–685, 689–697.
58. Marlborough; Battle of Blenheim, Aug. 13, 1704.	A. 276–278; M. 293, 294; B. 254, 256; C. 282, 283; T. 213; S. 156; G. 705–719; Gar. 657, 658, 676–685, 687–691, 695.
59. The Queen's Favorites; Sacheverell.	A. 279; M. 295, 296; B. 260; C. 286, 287; S. 157; G. 707, 716, 717; Gar. 677, 687, 690, 691.
60. Treaty of Utrecht, 1713.	A. 277; M. 297; B. 261; C. 285; T. 214; S. 156; G. 719; Gar. 696, 697.
61. Union of England and Scotland, 1707.	A. 278, 279; M. 298; B. 258; C. 285; T. 213, 214; S. 156; D. 306; G. 714, 715; Gar. 685.

62. Death of the Queen.

A. 279; M. 299; B. 262; C. 287; T. 215; S. 156; G. 720; Gar. 699–701.

SUPPLEMENTARY TOPICS ON THE STUART PERIOD.

1. Science and Invention: Royal Society of London, 1660; Greenwich Observatory; Sir Isaac Newton, 1642–1727.

A. 288; M. 268, 303; B. 218; T. 204; S. 151, 152; G. 609–611; Gar. 598, 623, 664; Br. 130–132.

2. Education; Books and Newspapers, 1641.

A. 268, 286, 289; M. 298, 299, 303; B. 249, 263; C. 278, 279, 295; T. 205, 209; S. 155; Gar. 663; E. 54, 55; Br. 108–117.

3. Architecture; Sir Christopher Wren.

A. 255, 288; M. 264, 303; T. 204; Gar. 631, 632, 662, 663, 665–668, 679, 681, 683, 700, 701.

4. The Quakers; George Fox; Pennsylvania, 1682.

A. 281, 282; B. 218; C. 355; T. 205; G. 660, 759; Gar. 629.

5. Origin of the Standing Army, 1661.

A. 267; B. 215; C. 244, 294; G. 619, 633, 689; Gar. 584.

6. Population.

A. 268, 284; C. 292, 293; S. 155; G. 765; Gar. 629.

7. Industry and Commerce.

A. 268, 282–286; M. 303, 304; B. 249, 250, 258; C. 293; T. 204; S. 154, 155; G. 699; Gar. 628, 664, 670, 671, 686, 687, 697, 698, 701.

8. Life, Manners, and Customs.

A. 280–282, 285, 287; M. 304; B. 234, 258; C. 294; T. 205; S. 155; Gar. 630–633; E. 39, 40, 49, 50.

PURITAN AND CLASSICAL LITERATURE.

1. John Milton, 1608–1674; *Paradise Lost.*

A. 261; M. 259; B. 217, 218, 263; C. 288, 289; T. 191; S. 141, 151; D. 252; G. 464–467, 526, 527, 531, 543, 544, 600–604, 662; Gar. 519, 546, 572, 596, 597; E. 39, 40, 44–46; Br. 117–123.

2. John Bunyan, 1628–1688 ;
   The Pilgrim's Progress.

   A. 261 ; M. 261 ; B. 217 ; C. 289, 290 ; S. 151 ; G. 467, 600, 625–628, 640, 670 ; Gar. 596–598 ; E. 47, 48 ; Br. 123, 124.

3. John Dryden, 1631–1700 ;
   Ode on St. Cecilia's Day.

   A. 362 ; M. 302 ; B. 226 ; C. 290 ; T. 191 ; G. 610, 637, 642 ; Gar. 623 ; E. 49, 50, 52, 53 ; Br. 125–130.

4. Daniel Defoe, 1661–1731 ;
   Robinson Crusoe.

   A. 307 ; M. 298, 299 ; B. 263 ; S. 163, 180 ; E. 56, 57 ; Br. 135, 139, 140.

5. Dean Swift, 1667–1745 ;
   Gulliver's Travels.

   A. 280, 307, 308 ; M. 298, 299 ; B. 263, 269 ; C. 349 ; S. 156, 180 ; Gar. 693, 695, 718 ; E. 57–59 ; Br. 139.

6. Joseph Addison, 1672–1719 ;
   The Spectator, 1711.

   A. 280 ; M. 298, 299 ; B. 263 ; C. 348 ; T. 215 ; S. 180 ; Gar. 692, 693 ; E. 60–62 ; Br. 141, 142.

7. Sir Richard Steele, 1672–1729 ;
   The Tatler, 1709.

   A. 280 ; B. 263 ; C. 348 ; T. 215 ; S. 180 ; E. 62, 63 ; Br. 141.

8. Alexander Pope, 1688–1744 ;
   Essay on Man.

   A. 280 ; C. 347 ; T. 215 ; Gar. 726 ; E. 59, 60 ; Br. 136, 137.

III. The House of Hanover. 1714 ——.

1. **George I.**, 1714–1727.

   A. 293; M. 306; B. 265; C. 297; T. 218; S. 162; D. 306; G. 721; Gar. 702.

2. Jacobite Rebellion of 1715.

   A. 293; M. 310; B. 266; C. 293, 300; S. 162; G. 725, 726; Gar. 704, 705.

3. Septennial Act, 1716.

   M. 311; B. 266; C. 300; S. 163; G. 725, 726; Gar. 706, 707.

4. The South Sea Bubble, 1720.

   A. 294; M. 311, 312; B. 267, 268; C. 301; T. 220; S. 163; G. 728; Gar. 711, 712.

5. Cabinet Government; Walpole Prime Minister, 1721.

   A. 295; M. 308, 313, 314; B. 262, 268, 269; C. 302; T. 221; S. 163; G. 696–698, 721–734; Gar. 627, 628, 647, 648, 659, 660, 673, 687, 688, 709–732, 739, 743, 744, 764.

6. **George II.**, 1727–1760.

   A. 296; M. 314; B. 270; C. 304; T. 220; S. 163; G. 730; Gar. 718.

7. The Spanish War, 1739.

   A. 297; M. 315; B. 271, 272; C. 307; T. 221; G. 732, 733; Gar. 729, 730.

8. War of the Austrian Succession, 1740–1748; Dettingen, June 27, 1743.

   A. 297–299; M. 316; B. 273; C. 307, 308; T. 221, 222; S. 164; G. 734, 741, 742; Gar. 732–739, 743.

9. Jacobite Rebellion of 1745; Culloden, April 16, 1746.

   A. 299–301; M. 316; B. 273, 274; C. 308, 309; T. 222, 223; S. 164; D. 306; G. 743, 744; Gar. 739–743.

18. Declaration of Independence, July 4, 1776. | A. 312 ; M. 328 ; B. 295 ; C. 321 ; S. 166; G. 778–780; Gar. 784.

19. Early Battles. | A. 312, 313 ; B. 294, 295 ; C. 321 ; T. 231, 232 ; S. 166 ; G. 779, 780 ; Gar. 782–786.

20. Surrender of Burgoyne at Saratoga, Oct. 17, 1777; French Aid for the Colonies, 1778. | A. 313 ; B. 296 ; C. 322 ; T. 232 ; G. 781, 782 ; Gar. 786–788.

21. Surrender of Cornwallis at Yorktown, Oct. 19, 1781 ; George Washington. | A. 313 ; M. 329 ; B. 297 ; C. 323 ; T. 233 ; G. 779, 785 ; Gar. 792, 794.

22. The Colonies Independent ; Peace of Paris, Sept. 3, 1783. | A. 313 ; M. 329 ; B. 298 ; C. 323 ; T. 234 ; S. 167 ; G. 786 ; Gar. 783, 784, 794–798.

23. The Gordon Riots, 1780. | A. 335 ; M. 330 ; B. 297 ; Gar. 789–792.

24. Trial of Warren Hastings, Feb. 13, 1788–April 23, 1795. | A. 315, 316 ; M. 330 ; B. 299–301 ; C. 324, 325 ; T. 235 ; S. 167, 168 ; G. 783–785, 789, 795, 796 ; Gar. 801–811.

25. Burke, Fox, Sheridan, the Younger Pitt. | A. 312, 316, 323 ; M. 332, 337, 361 ; B. 273, 303 ; C. 325, 326 ; T. 235, 236, 238, 239 ; S. 168 ; G. 770–772, 786–797, 799–818, 820–822, 825 ; Gar. 772, 780, 789, 790, 795, 799–801, 804, 806–812, 819, 822–835, 840, 842, 843, 846, 848, 855, 856 ; · E. 75, 76 ; Br. 152, 153.

26. Law and Prison Reforms ; Bentham, Howard, Elizabeth Fry. | A. 298 ; M. 331, 332 ; B. 312 ; S. 176, 177 ; G. 739–741, 829 ; Gar. 890, 939 ; Br. 155.

27. Abolition of the Slave Trade, 1772–1807; Wilberforce and Clarkson.

A. 350, 351; M. 332; B. 312, 313; C. 362, 363; T. 248; G. 395, 737, 740, 796, 797, 823; Gar. 823, 857.

28. Union of England and Ireland, 1800.

A. 319; M. 337; B. 306, 309, 310; C. 330; T. 236, 237; S. 168; D. 307; G. 794, 795, 811–818; Gar. 795, 796, 810, 831–834, 840–843.

29. England in the French Revolution: Battle of the Nile, Aug. 1, 1798.

A. 317, 318; M. 332, 333; B. 307–309; C. 328; T. 236, 237; S. 169; G. 798–811; Gar. 820–830, 834–838.

30. Trafalgar, Oct. 21, 1805.

A. 321, 322; M. 333; B. 311; C. 329; T. 238, 239; S. 169; G. 820–822; Gar. 851–854.

31. The English in Portugal and Spain.

A. 324–327; M. 334; B. 314–316; C. 331–334; T. 240; S. 170; G. 824–827, 832; Gar. 862–867, 871, 872.

32. Waterloo, June 18, 1815. (End of the Second Hundred Years' War of England and France, 1702–1815.)

A. 329; M. 335, 336; B. 317, 318; C. 335, 336; T. 243; S. 171; G. 830–832, 834–836; Gar. 874.

33. Napoleon, Nelson, Wellington.

A. 317, 318, 322, 325; M. 333–336; B. 309, 318, 331; C. 327, 328, 331–336; T. 237–240, 243; S. 169–172; G. 810, 811, 818–836, 839; Gar. 826, 834, 837–840, 844, 845, 848–875, 893, 896, 900, 938.

34. The War of 1812.

A. 327, 328; M. 334, 335; B. 313; C. 334; T. 242, 243; S. 172; G. 827–830, 832–834; Gar. 872, 873.

35. Condition of the Country after these Wars.	A. 330; M. 336; B. 318, 319; T. 244; S. 175, 176; G. 837; Gar. 875–879.
36. Prince of Wales Regent, 1810–1820; Death of **George III.**	A. 330; M. 343; B. 319, 320; C. 332, 337; T. 241–245; S. 172; G. 838; Gar. 811, 812, 868.
37. **George IV.**, 1820–1830.	A. 344; M. 344; B. 322; C. 338; T. 246; S. 183; G. 838; Gar. 880.
38. Discontent and Conspiracy.	A. 345; M. 344, 345; B. 322–327; C. 338; G. 837, 838; Gar. 879–881.
39. Queen Caroline ; Brougham.	A. 345, 346; M. 346; B. 322; C. 339; S. 183; Gar. 881, 882.
40. Reforms ; Canning and O'Connell.	A. 348, 355; M. 347; B. 324–330; T. 246; S. 189; G. 823–826, 829, 838–841; Gar. 857, 865, 882–887, 891–896.
41. Independence of Greece, 1827 (Byron).	A. 347; B. 323; C. 340; T. 246; S. 184; G. 838; Gar. 884, 892, 893.
42. **William IV.**, 1830–1837.	A. 348; M. 349; B. 330; C. 341; T. 347; S. 184; D. 307; G. 840; Gar. 898.
43. Parliamentary Reform, 1832; Radicals, Liberals, Conservatives ; Cobbett and Russell.	A. 330–333, 348; M. 349–353; B. 330–333; C. 338, 342; T. 228, 247, 248; S. 185; G. 837–843; Gar. 877, 879, 891, 893–905, 912, 913, 932–934, 937, 961, 962, 972.
44. Abolition of Slavery, 1833; Factory Reform.	A. 350, 351; M. 354, 355; B. 333, 334; C. 342; T. 248; S. 185; G. 833; Gar. 876, 877, 910, 911, 927.

45. **Victoria, 1837 ——.** (A Reign of Peace and Progress.)

A. 351; M. 357; B. 337; C. 343; T. 248, 250; S. 187; D. 307; G. 840; Gar. 914.

46. Her Marriage to Prince Albert, Feb. 10, 1840.

A. 353; M. 362; B. 341; C. 343; T. 251; S. 187; Gar. 920.

47. The Chartists.

A. 356; M. 363–365; B. 340, 345; C. 343; T. 250, 251; S. 188; Gar. 922–924, 935, 936.

48. Famine in Ireland.

M. 366, 367; B. 343; C. 344; T. 250, 251; S. 189; G. 841; Gar. 931–933.

49. Repeal of the Corn Laws, 1838–1849; Peel, Cobden, Bright.

A. 353, 356; M. 365–368; B. 334, 340–345; C. 340, 344; T. 244, 246, 248, 250; S. 188, 205; G. 837–842; Gar. 875, 876, 879, 885, 887, 891–895, 912, 913, 924–932, 936, 955, 958.

50. The World's Fair of 1851.

A. 357; M. 368; B. 347; T. 252; S. 189; Gar. 937.

51. Death of the Prince Consort, 1861.

A. 365; M. 370; B. 357; T. 264; S. 190; Gar. 959.

52. American Civil War; the Alabama Claims.

M. 371, 372; B. 356; T. 264, 265; S. 198; G. 843; Gar. 958–960, 965, 966.

53. Lord Palmerston.

A. 359; B. 344, 348–350, 355; T. 247, 254; G. 840, 842, 843; Gar. 901, 912, 938, 939, 945, 947, 955, 956, 960.

54. Further Parliamentary Reform, 1867 and 1886.

A. 364; M. 373, 374; B. 355; S. 204; G. 843, 844; Gar. 961, 962, 972.

55. Disestablishment of the Irish Episcopal Church, 1869; Abolition of Compulsory Church Rates.

A. 364; M. 374, 375; B. 358; C. 346; S. 197; G. 844; Gar. 962.

56. Education Act, 1870.

A. 365; M. 375; B. 358, 359; C. 346; T. 270; S. 197; G. 840, 844; Gar. 920, 963, 965.

57. Irish Land Acts; the Land League.

A. 368–370; M. 376–378; B. 359, 360; C. 346; T. 268, 269; S. 197, 204; Gar. 962, 963, 970, 971.

58. The Phœnix Park Assassination, May 6, 1882.

A. 369, 370; M. 378; B. 360; T. 268; Gar. 970.

59. Home Rule for Ireland.

A. 375; B. 360; T. 269; S. 204; Gar. 970; *Cent.*, vol. 4, 249–264; vol. 15, 317, 318; *Harper*, vol. 75, 421–429; *Forum*, vol. 5, 331–340.

60. Disraeli; Salisbury; Parnell.

A. 369, 374–376, 387; M. 373; B. 359, 360; C. 346; T. 265–268; S. 204, 205; G. 843, 844; Gar. 929–931, 938, 939, 956, 961, 962, 966, 969, 970, 972; *Scrib.*, vol. 14, 190–194; vol. 22, 262–265; *Cent.*, vol. 1, 729–744, 939–942; *Harper*, vol. 34, 753–758; vol. 36, 800–809; vol. 65, 163–184; vol. 70, 339–349.

61. The Queen's Jubilee, 1887; the Prince of Wales.

A. 375; B. 354, 357; T. 271; S. 198, 221; *Forum*, vol. 4, 166–176; *Harper*, vol. 70, 745–773.

62. William Ewart Gladstone; Prime Minister, 1868–1874, 1880–1885, 1886, 1892–1894.

A. 368, 388; M. 362, 374; B. 355, 360; C. 346; T. 266–269; S. 204; G. 844; Gar. 926, 943, 955, 956, 958, 962–966, 970, 972; *Harper*, vol. 33, 61–64 ; vol. 64, 741–751 ; *Scrib.*, vol. 21, 125–138 ; *Forum*, vol. 4, 553–560 ; vol. 8, 1–17 ; *R. of Rs.*, vol. 9, 416–422, 429–433.

63. The Earl of Rosebery Prime Minister, March 3, 1894 ——.

R. of Rs., vol. 9, 422–428 ; *Forum*, vol. 17, 139–147.

SUPPLEMENTARY TOPICS ON THE HANOVERIAN PERIOD.

1. Rebellion in Canada, 1837–1840.

A. 352; T. 250; S. 190; G. 840; Gar. 914, 916.

2. The Opium War, 1839–1842.

A. 354; M. 369; B. 342; T. 258-260; S. 193, 194; G. 840.

3. War in the Crimea, 1854–1856; Siege of Sebastopol; Florence Nightingale.

A. 357–361; M. 369–370; B. 349, 350; C. 344; T. 252-255; S. 195, 196; G. 842; Gar. 943-948.

4. The Sepoy Rebellion, 1857–1859; Memorable Sieges; End of East India Company; Victoria Empress of India, 1877.

A. 361, 362; M. 370; B. 351–354; C. 344-346; T. 256-258; S. 191-193; G. 842, 843; Gar. 948-955.

5. The Soudan, 1884–1885; General Gordon.

A. 372–374; B. 354-362; T. 267; S. 203, 204; Gar. 971; *Cent.*, vol. 6, 556–561.

6. Other Wars.

A. 353-355, 357, 363, 364, 366, 367, 371, 372, 376; B. 342, 343, 354; C. 344, 345; T. 260, 265-267; S. 190, 191, 194, 199-203; G. 840, 842; Gar. 956, 957, 970, 971.

7. Social and National Progress; Discovery and Invention (Watt and Arkwright); Steam Railway, 1830; Electric Telegraph, 1837; Atlantic Cable, 1858.

A. 336–342, 380, 381; M. 338–341, 355, 356, 368, 380–383; B. 321, 335–337, 339, 356–363; T. 244, 270, 271; S. 179, 182, 183, 185, 206; G. 735–741, 791, 792, 797, 828, 829, 837–844; Gar. 708, 813–818, 884–886, 905–911, 916–918, 932, 933, 939, 940.

8. Commerce and Navigation.

A. 336; M. 340, 341; B. 361; S. 178; G. 729, 791–795, 822, 823, 828, 829, 837, 841; Gar. 722–728, 751, 860, 885–887, 936, 958.

9. Population, Land, and Rents.

A. 7; M. 361, 408; B. 360; T. 228; S. 183, 205, 211; G. 791, 828; Gar. 813, 817, 933; *Forum*, vol. 18, 161, 162.

10. The Postal Service; Police.

A. 285; M. 348, 363; B. 191, 334, 339; C. 294; S. 140, 155, 197; Gar. 900, 901, 918, 920.

11. The Gregorian Calendar, 1752.

M. 318, 319; B. 295; C. 315; S. 182; Gar. 743.

12. Periodicals.

A. 381; M. 342; C. 295; T. 257, 270; S. 174; G. 767, 775, 776, 829; Gar. 722, 773, 779; E. 81; Br. 146, 153, 154.

13. Art and Music.

A. 340, 341; M. 342, 380; B. 322; S. 166, 174; Gar. 943, 946; E. 135.

14. Travel and Exploration: Sir John Franklin; David Livingstone; Henry M. Stanley.

A. 365; M. 379; B. 362; *Scrib.*, vol. 7, 662–692; vol. 8, 210–222; Br. 155.

15. The British Constitution: House of Lords; House of Commons.

A. ap. 1–4; M. 358–362, 380; B. 248–262; T. 272–274; S. 208, 209; G. 231, 232, 536; Gar. 695, 710, 914; *Forum*, vol. 8, 531–541; vol. 17, 329–339; *Harper*, vol. 73, 505–517; *Scrib.*, vol. 14, 593–600.

16. Rise of the English People; Unity of the English-speaking Race.

M. 383–390; B. 362–364; T. 234; S. 206, 207; G. 2–16, 787.

CLASSICAL, ROMANTIC, AND VICTORIAN LITERATURE.

1. Novelists: Richardson; Fielding; Sterne; Smollett.

A. 344 ; S. 173, 180 ; Gar. 746 ; E. 63–68 ; Br. 145–149.

2. Samuel Johnson, 1709–1784; *English Dictionary.*

A. 344 ; M. 290 ; B. 321 ; C. 350 ; S. 173 ; E. 69–72 ; Br. 147.

3. David Hume, 1711–1776 ; *History of England.*

A. 344 ; S. 173 ; E. 72 ; Br. 150, 151.

4. Thomas Gray, 1716-1771; S. 173; Gar. 755; Br. 163.
   *Elegy in a Country Church-
   yard.*

5. Adam Smith, 1723-1790; B. 301, 302; G. 792, 793; Gar.
   The Wealth of Nations. 810; E. 76; Br. 151, 152.

6. Oliver Goldsmith, 1728- A. 343; B. 321; C. 350; S. 173;
   1774; E. 76-78; Br. 149, 163.
   The Vicar of Wakefield.

7. William Cowper, 1731-1800; A. 343; B. 321; S. 173; E. 80-
   The Task. 83; Br. 166-168.

8. Edward Gibbon, 1737-1794; A. 344; B. 321; E. 73, 74; Br.
   Decline and Fall of the 150.
   Roman Empire.

9. Richard Brinsley Sheridan, A. 316; B. 321; C. 325; S. 168,
   1751-1816; 173; Gar. 811; E. 79; Br.
   The Rivals. 144.

10. Robert Burns, 1759-1796; A. 343; S. 173; Gar. 887, 888;
    The Cotter's Saturday Night. E. 84, 85; Br. 168, 169.

11. William Wordsworth, 1770- A. 383; S. 206; Gar. 889; E.
    1850; 90-92; Br. 170-175.
    The Excursion.

12. Sir Walter Scott, 1771-1832; A. 383; S. 173, 186; Gar. 889;
    Waverley Novels. E. 94-97; Br. 156-158, 175.

13. Samuel Taylor Coleridge, A. 383; S. 173; Gar. 918, 920;
    1772-1834; E. 88, 89; B. 155, 171.
    The Ancient Mariner.

14. Thomas Campbell, 1777- A. 383; E. 92, 93; Br. 175.
    1844;
    War Songs.

15. Charles Lamb, 1775-1834; A. 385; E. 102; Br. 154.
    Essays of Elia.

16. Thomas Moore, 1779-1852; A. 382; S. 206; E. 93, 94; Br.
    Lalla Rookh. 176.

17. Thomas De Quincey, 1785–1859; *Confessions of an English Opium-Eater.*

A. 385; E. 104, 105.

18. Lord Byron, 1788–1824; *Childe Harold's Pilgrimage.*

A. 347, 382; S. 173, 184; Gar. 888; E. 85–87; Br. 177, 178.

19. Percy Bysshe Shelley, 1792–1822; *Lyrics.*

A. 382; Gar. 888, 889; E. 97, 98; Br. 178–181.

20. John Keats, 1795–1821; *Lyrics.*

A. 382; E. 98, 99; B. 181–183.

21. Thomas Carlyle, 1795–1881; *Heroes and Hero-Worship.*

A. 388; M. 380; B. 362; S. 206; Gar. 941; E. 106–108, 120–122.

22. Thomas Babington Macaulay, 1800–1859; *Essays.*

A. 386; M. 380; B. 362; S. 206; Gar. 903, 904, 941; E. 118–120.

23. Sir E. G. E. L. Bulwer-Lytton, 1805–1873; *The Last Days of Pompeii.*

A. 386; E. 113.

24. Alfred Tennyson, 1809–1892; *Idyls of the King.*

A. 385; M. 361, 380; B. 362; Gar. 943; E. 133–135; Br. 184, 185.

25. Elizabeth Barrett Browning, 1809–1861; *Aurora Leigh.*

A. 385; E. 129–131.

26. Robert Browning, 1812–1889; *Pippa Passes.*

A. 385; E. 131–133; Br. 183, 184.

27. William Makepeace Thackeray, 1811–1863; *Vanity Fair.*

A. 387; M. 380; B. 362; S. 206; Gar. 940, 941; E. 108, 109.

28. Charles Dickens, 1812–1870; *David Copperfield.*

A. 387; Gar. 940; E. 110, 111.

29. Charlotte Brontë, 1816–1855;   A. 387; E. 112.
Jane Eyre.

30. Charles Kingsley, 1819–1875;   A. 387; E. 114.
Hypatia.

31. John Ruskin, 1819 ——;   A. 388; M. 380; B. 362; E. 125–127.
Modern Painters.

32. George Eliot, 1820–1880;   A. 386; E. 115, 116.
Adam Bede.

33. Matthew Arnold, 1822–1888;   A. 386; S. 206; E. 123, 124.
Essays in Criticism.

34. Jean Ingelow, 1830 ——;   A. 385.
Songs of Seven.

35. William Morris, 1834 ——;   E. 136; *Cent.*, vol. 10, 388–397.
The Earthly Paradise.

36. Algernon Charles Swinburne, 1837 ——;   A. 386; E. 136, 137.
Mary Stuart.

37. John Richard Green, 1837–1883;   B. 362; G. Introduction.
History of the English People.

38. Scientific and Philosophical Writers and Thinkers: John Stuart Mill (1806–1873); Herbert Spencer (1820 ——); Sir John W. F. Herschel (1792–1871); Sir Charles Lyell (1797–1875); Hugh Miller (1802–1856); John Tyndall (1820–1893); Charles Darwin (1809–1882); Thomas H. Huxley (1825 ——); Richard A. Proctor (1837–1888).   A. 388, 389; M. 378–380; B. 361, 362; S. 206; Gar. 940, 941; E. 127–129; Br. 155.

COLONIES OF THE BRITISH EMPIRE.

1. European.[1]

A. ap. 4, 5 ; M 294 ; B. 261, 363 ; C. 74, 284, 323, 337 ; T. 213, 214, 238, 240 ; S. 210 ; G. 818, 837 ; Gar. 696, 848, 970.

2. Asiatic.

A. ap. 5–8 ; M. 317, 318, 369 ; B. 169, 276, 277, 305, 345, 346, 353, 354, 363 ; C. 324, 325 ; T. 160, 164, 225, 256–259 ; S. 115, 165, 190–193, 210 ; G. 396, 745, 746, 753, 754, 764, 782–785, 789, 795, 796, 809, 837, 842, 843 ; Gar. 758–764, 801–808, 858, 859, 948–955.

3. African.

A. ap. 9–11 ; B. 305, 327, 346, 359, 363 ; C. 371–374 ; S. 211 ; G. 809, 837 ; Gar. 837, 858, 966–970.

4. Australian and Polynesian.

A. ap. 8, 9 ; B. 298, 299, 327, 328, 346, 347, 363 ; C. 374–380 ; T. 260–263 ; S. 211 ; Gar. 858, 967, 968.

5. North American.

A. ap. 11, 12 ; B. 261, 278, 282, 283, 327, 338, 339 ; C. 351 ; 363, 365–370 ; T. 214 ; S. 190, 211 ; G. 755–757, 764, 802, 833, 840 ; Gar. 696, 753–756, 766, 784, 914, 916, 966, 967.

6. West Indian.

A. ap. 12 ; B. 210, 211, 363 ; C. 357–363 ; T. 188, 214, 238, 240 ; S. 211 ; G. 593, 764, 809, 837 ; Gar. 572, 837, 859, 966, 967.

7. South American.

A. ap. 13 ; B. 363 ; C. 363, 364 ; T. 262 ; S. 211 ; Gar. 858.

[1] For Colonies see *Forum,* vol. 18, 161–172.

ADDITIONAL READING AND REFERENCE.

I. PREHISTORIC BRITAIN.

Early Man in Britain	*W. B. Dawkins.*
Celtic Britain	*J. Rhys.*
The Dawn of History	*C. F. Keary.*
Origins of English History	*C. J. Elton.*

II. ROMAN BRITAIN.

Roman Britain	*H. M. Scarth.*
The Romans in Britain	*H. C. Coote.*
The Celt, the Roman, and the Saxon	*T. Wright.*
Gallic War (Books IV. and V.)	*Julius Cæsar.*

III. ANGLO-SAXON BRITAIN.

The Making of England	*J. R. Green.*
Anglo-Saxon Britain	*G. Allen.*
Early English History	*E. A. Freeman.*
The Saxons in England	*J. M. Kemble.*
Alfred the Great	*R. Pauli.*
Alfred the Great	*T. Hughes.*
Morte D'Arthur	*Sir T. Malory.*
Idyls of the King	*A. Tennyson.*
Vision of Sir Launfal	*J. R. Lowell.*
Macbeth	*W. Shakespeare.*

IV. THE NORMAN CONQUEST.

History of the Norman Conquest	*E. A. Freeman.*
The Normans in Europe	*A. H. Johnson.*
William the Conqueror	*J. Abbott.*
The Age of Chivalry	*T. Bulfinch.*

The Crusades . . . . *G. W. Cox.*
The Children's Crusade . . . . *G. Z. Gray.*
St. Anselm . . . . *R. W. Church.*
Hereward, the Last of the English . . . . *C. Kingsley.*
Harold the Dauntless; The Betrothed . . . . *Sir W. Scott.*
Harold . . . . *A. Tennyson.*
Harold . . . . *Sir E. G. Bulwer-Lytton.*
In His Name . . . . *E. E. Hale.*

V. THE PLANTAGENETS.

The Early Plantagenets . . . . *W. Stubbs.*
England under the Angevin Kings . . . . *Miss K. Norgate.*
The Rise of the People . . . . *J. Rowley.*
Edward III. . . . . *W. Warburton.*
Richard I. . . . . *J. Abbott.*
Simon de Montfort . . . . *M. Creighton.*
John Wycliffe . . . . *L. Sergeant.*
The Canterbury Tales . . . . *G. Chaucer.*
King John; Richard II. . . . . *W. Shakespeare.*
Ivanhoe ; The Talisman ; Castle Dangerous ; Tales
 of a Grandfather . . . . *Sir W. Scott.*
The Scottish Chiefs . . . . *Miss J. Porter.*

VI. LANCASTER AND YORK.

Houses of Lancaster and York . . . . *J. Gairdner.*
Richard III. . . . . *J. Gairdner.*
Wars of the Roses . . . . *J. G. Edgar.*
Henry V. . . . . *G. M. Towle.*
Joan of Arc . . . . *J. Michelet.*
Henry IV.; V.; VI.; Richard III. . . . . . . *W. Shakespeare.*
Fair Maid of Perth ; Anne of Geierstein ; Quentin
 Durward . . . . *Sir W. Scott.*
Last of the Barons . . . . *Sir E. G. Bulwer-Lytton.*

VII. THE TUDORS.

The Age of Elizabeth . . . . *M. Creighton.*
The Tudors and the Reformation . . . . *M. Creighton.*
The Era of the Protestant Revolution . . . . . . *F. Seebohm.*

VIII. The Stuarts.

IX. The House of Hanover.

The Colonial Era . . . . *G. P. Fisher.*
Life of Gladstone . . . . *W. Clark Russell.*
England under Gladstone . . . . *J. H. McCarthy.*
England Without and Within . . . . *R. G. White.*
English Traits . . . . *R. W. Emerson.*
English Statesmen . . . . *T. W. Higginson.*
Our Old Home ; American and English Note-Books *N. Hawthorne.*
One Hundred Days in Europe . . . . *O. W. Holmes.*
Tom Brown's School Days ; Tom Brown at Oxford . *T. Hughes.*
Rob Roy ; Waverley ; Heart of Midlothian ; Red
   Gauntlet ; Guy Mannering . . . . *Sir W. Scott.*
The Virginians ; Vanity Fair . . . . *W. M. Thackeray.*
The Vicar of Wakefield . . . . *O. Goldsmith.*
Barnaby Rudge ; Oliver Twist ; Tale of Two Cities ;
   Bleak House . . . . *C. Dickens.*
Adam Bede ; Middlemarch . . . . *George Eliot.*

X. GENERAL WORKS.

Old English Chronicles . . . . ————
History of the English People . . . . *J. R. Green.*
History of England (1603–1642) ; A School Atlas of
   English History ; Outline of English History . . *S. R. Gardiner.*
History of England ; Essays . . . . *T. B. Macaulay.*
History of England . . . . *D. Hume.*
History of England . . . . *J. Lingard.*
Pictorial History of England . . . . *C. Knight.*
Childhood of the English Nation . . . . *Miss E. S. Armitage.*
Lectures on the History of England . . . . . . *M. J. Guest.*
Lectures on Modern History . . . . *T. Arnold.*
Queens of England . . . . *Miss A. Strickland.*
History of the Nineteenth Century . . . . *R. Mackenzie.*
Student's Summary of English History . . . . . *T. Haughton.*
Church of England . . . . *R. W. Dixon.*
Middle Ages . . . . *H. Hallam.*
Domestic Manners in England during the Middle Ages *T. Wright.*
Growth of English Industry and Commerce . . . . *W. Cunningham.*
House of Commons . . . . *R. F. D. Palgrave.*
English Government and Constitution . . . . . . *J. Russell.*
Constitutional History of England . . . . *T. P. Taswell-Langmead.*
English Constitution . . . . *W. Bagehot.*

Constitutional History of England (—— 1485) . . *W. Stubbs.*
(1485–1760) . . *H. Hallam.*
(1760–1860) . . *T. E. May.*
Outline of Irish History . . . . *J. H. McCarthy.*
History of the United States . . . . *G. Bancroft.*
Old South Leaflets (historical documents) . . . . *Edited by E. D. Mead.*
Origins and History of the English Language . . . *G. P. Marsh.*
Origins of the English People and of the English
  Language . . . . *J. Roemer.*
Development of English Literature and Language . *A. H. Welsh.*
Cyclopedia of English Literature . . . . *W. and R. Chambers.*
History of Elizabethan Literature . . . . *G. Saintsbury.*
Literature of the Age of Elizabeth . . . . *E. P. Whipple.*
History of English Literature. . . . . *H. A. Taine.*
History of Eighteenth-Century Literature . . . . *E. W. Gosse.*
Victorian Poets . . . . *E. C. Stedman.*
English Men of Letters Series . . . . *Edited by J. Morley.*

FOR FURTHER REFERENCE :

Manual of Historical Literature (pp. 465–565) . . . *C. K. Adams.*
Reader's Guide to English History . . . . *W. F. Allen.*
Methods of Teaching and Studying History . . . . *Edited by G. S. Hall.*

INDEX.

www.ingramcontent.com/pod-product-compliance
Lightning Source LLC
Chambersburg PA
CBHW020242090426
42735CB00010B/1808